The helpful bulldozer

Story by Jenny Giles
Illustrations by Craig Smith

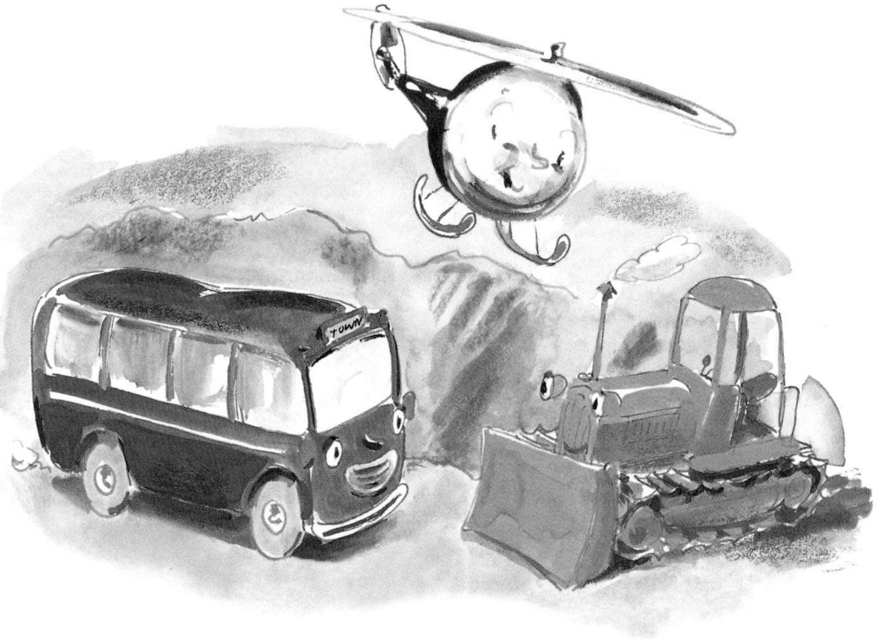
TOWN

The blue bus
went up the road to town.

The helicopter saw the bus.
He came flying down.

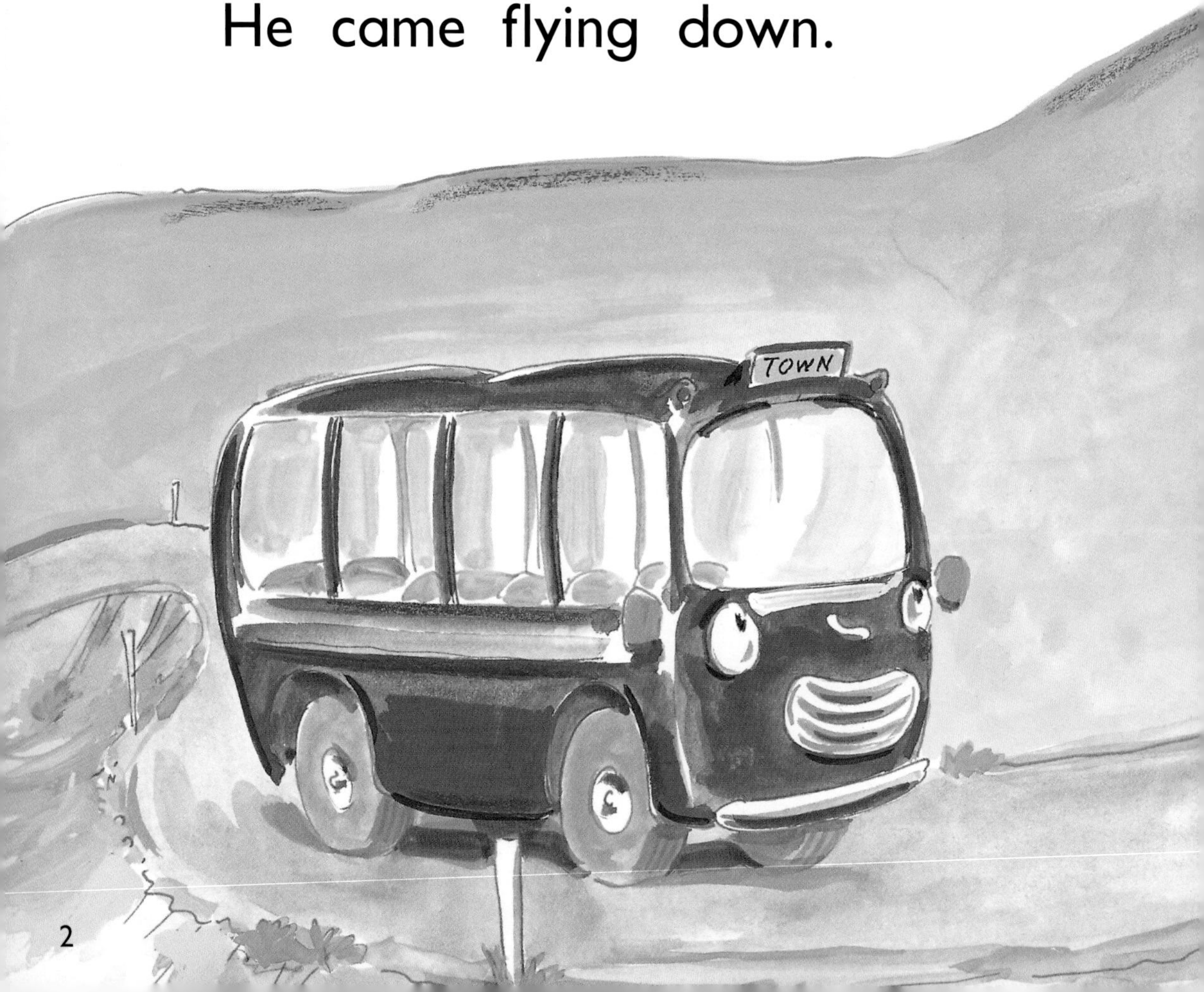
TOWN

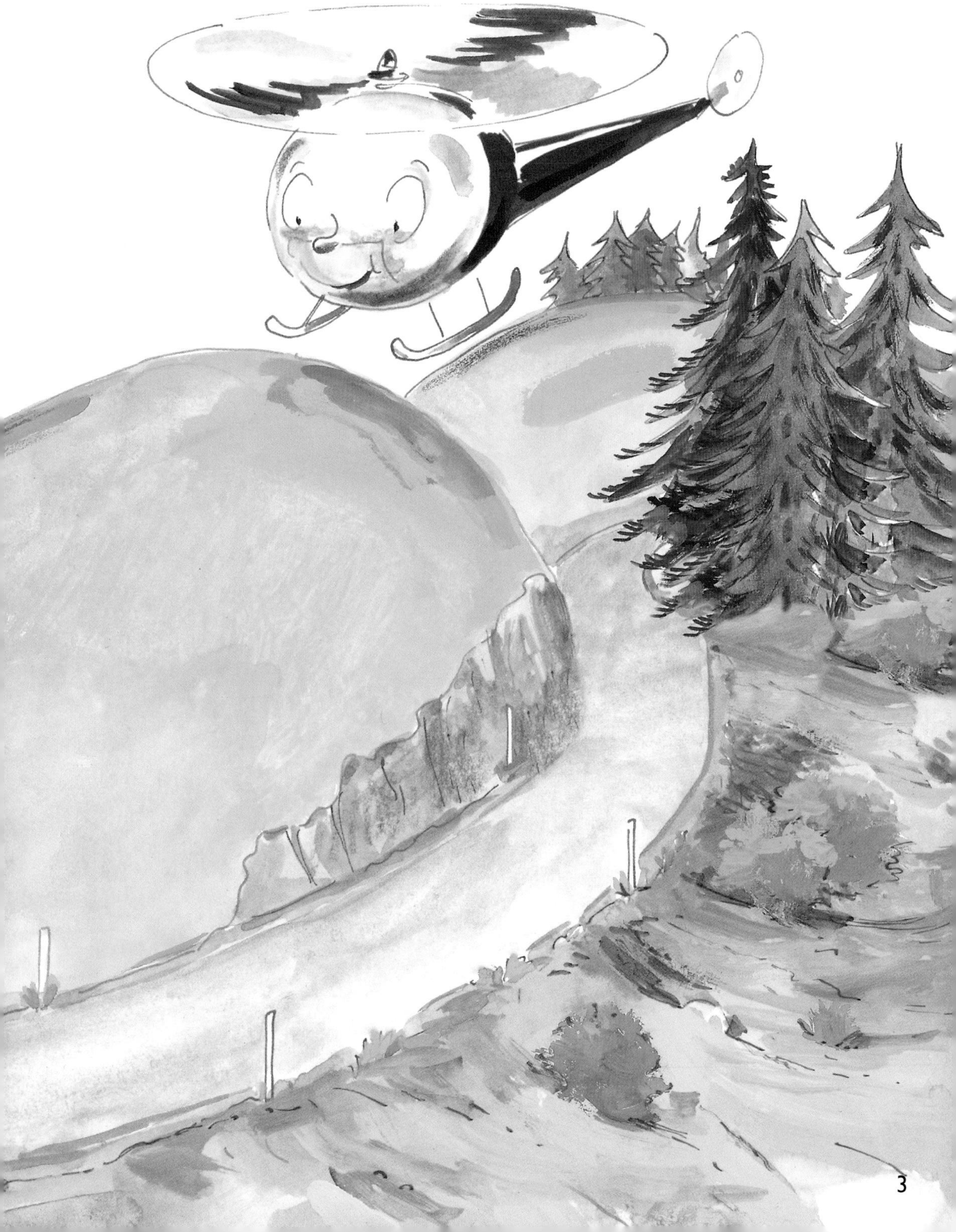

"A tree has come down
on the road by the big hill,"
said the helicopter.
"You can't go to town today!"

"But I **have** to go to town,"
said the bus.

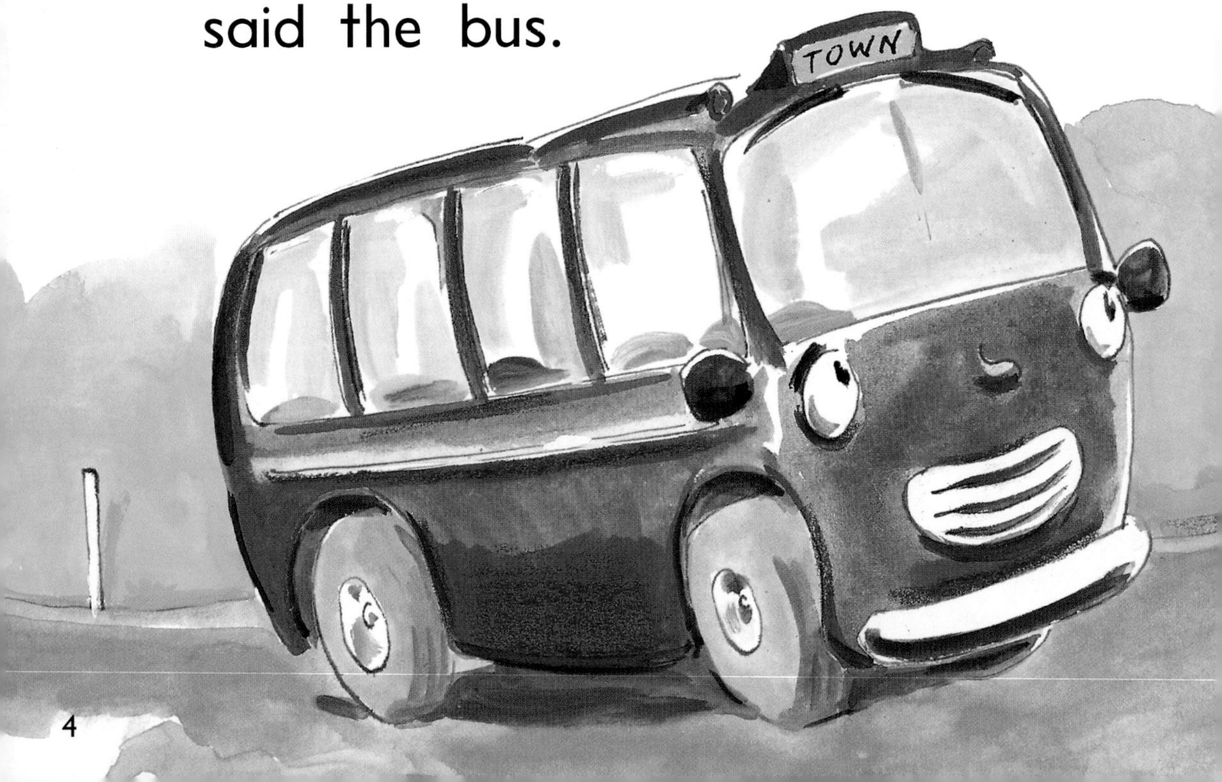
TOWN

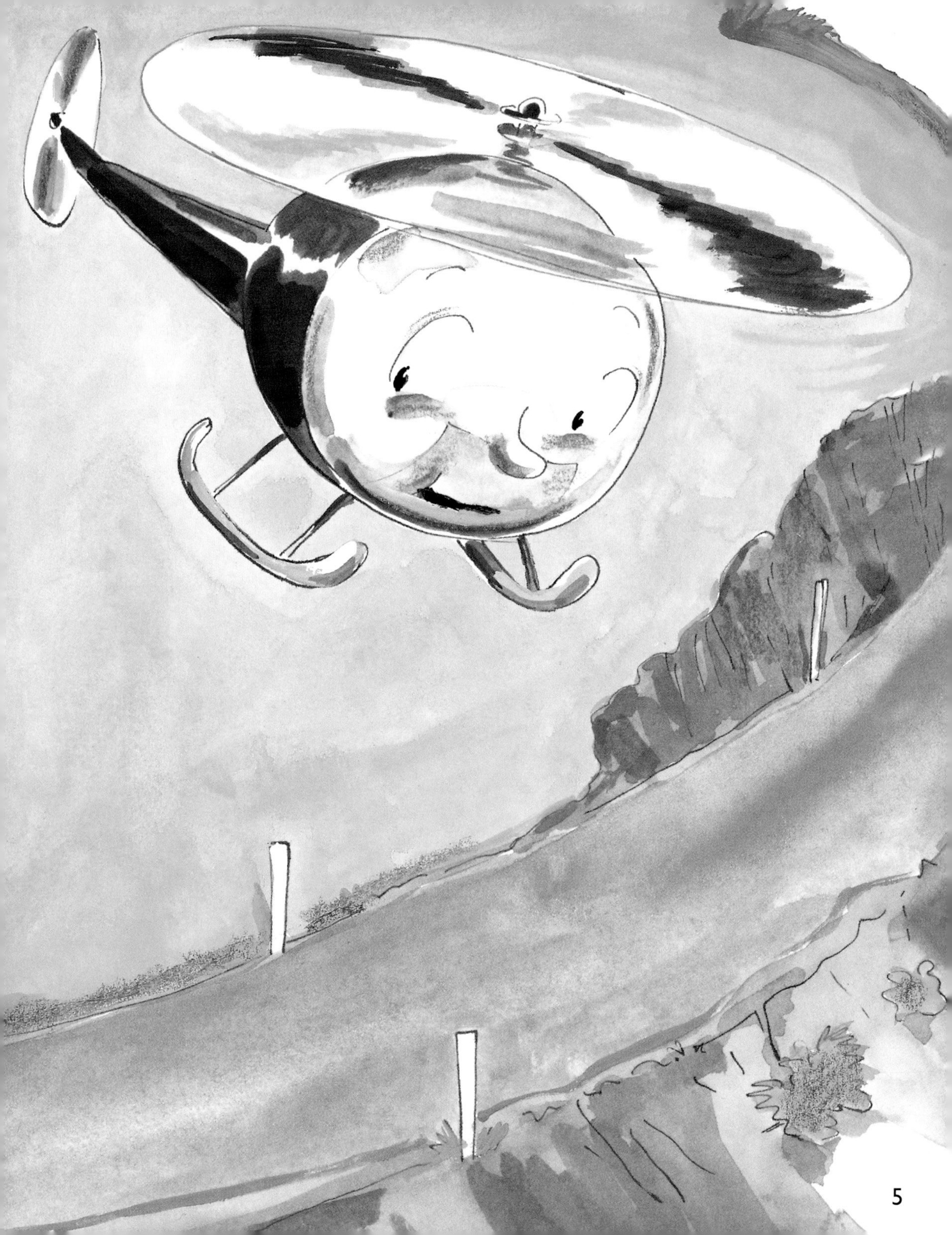

"Come and have a look
at the tree,"
said the helicopter.
"I will show you where it is."

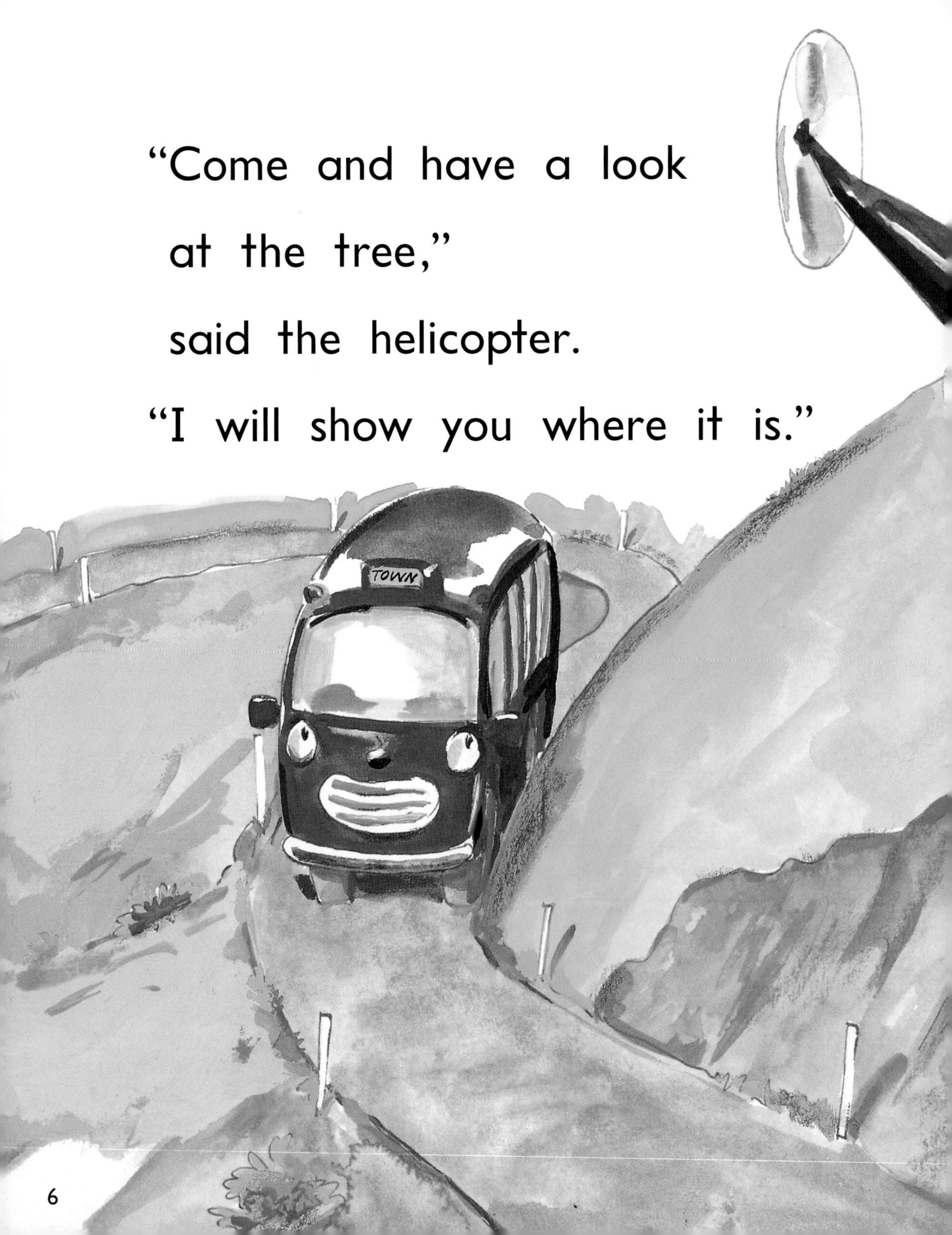
TOWN

They went to see the tree.

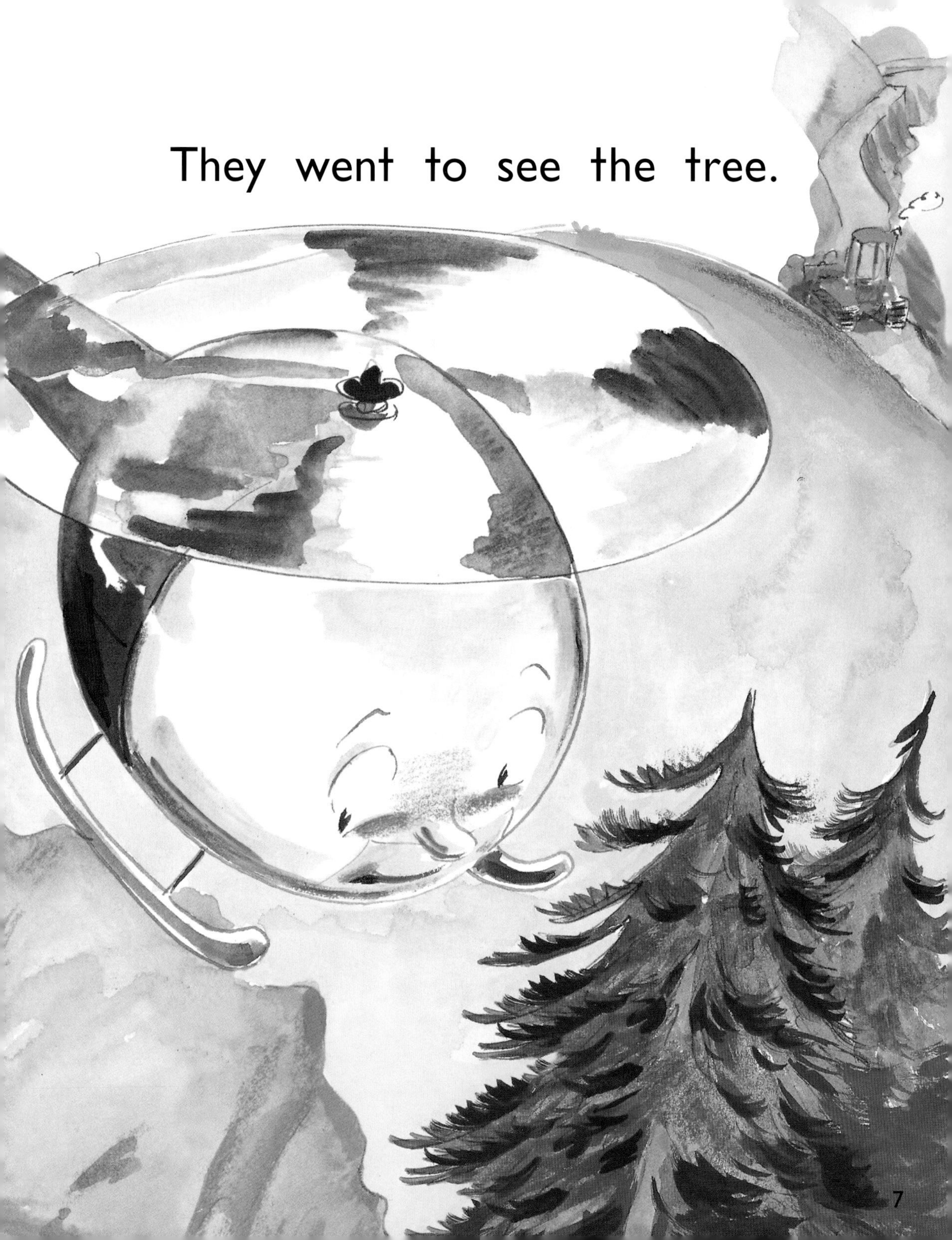

"Oh, yes!" said the bus.
"That tree **is** in my way.
Who can help me?"

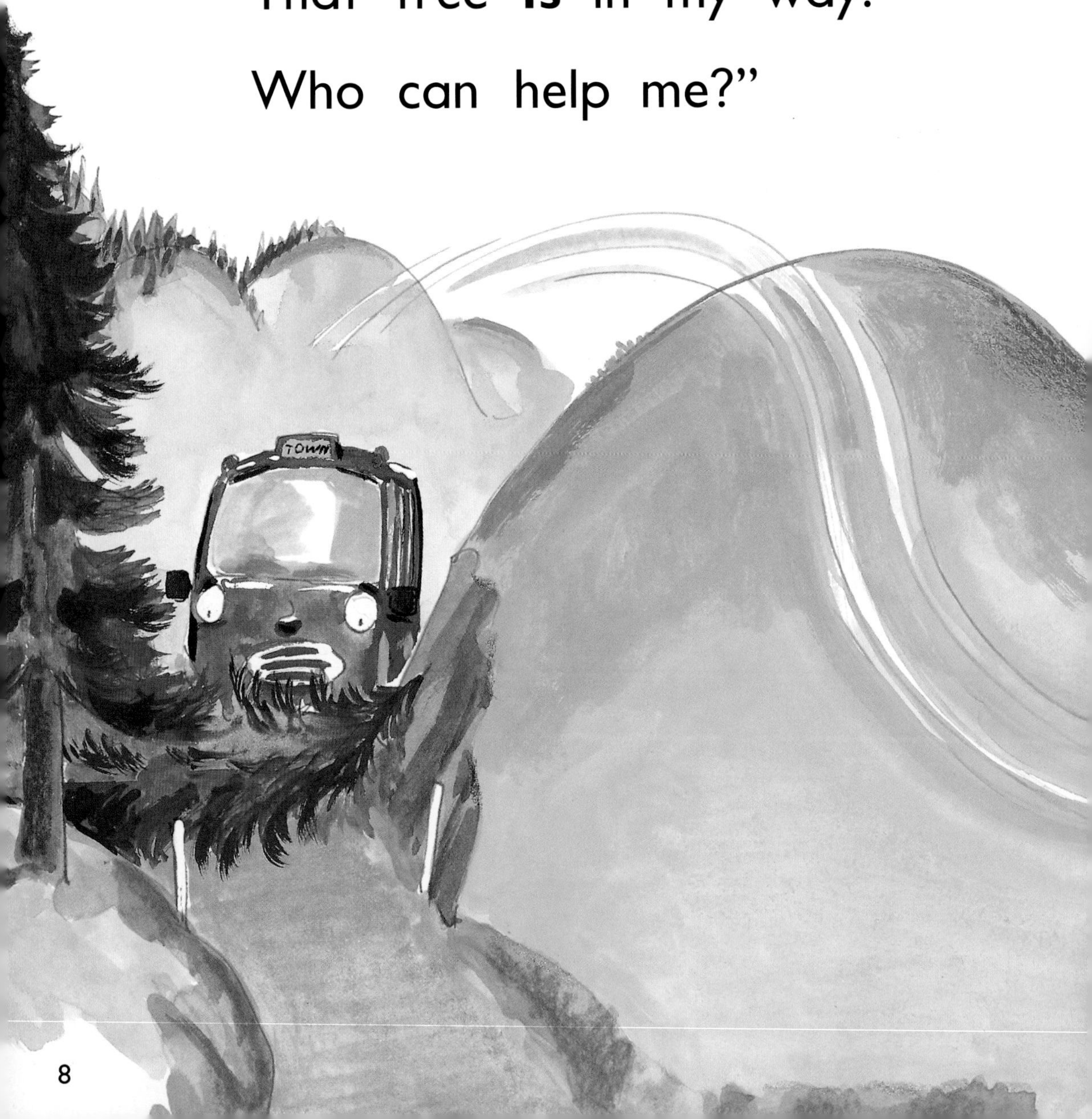
TOWN

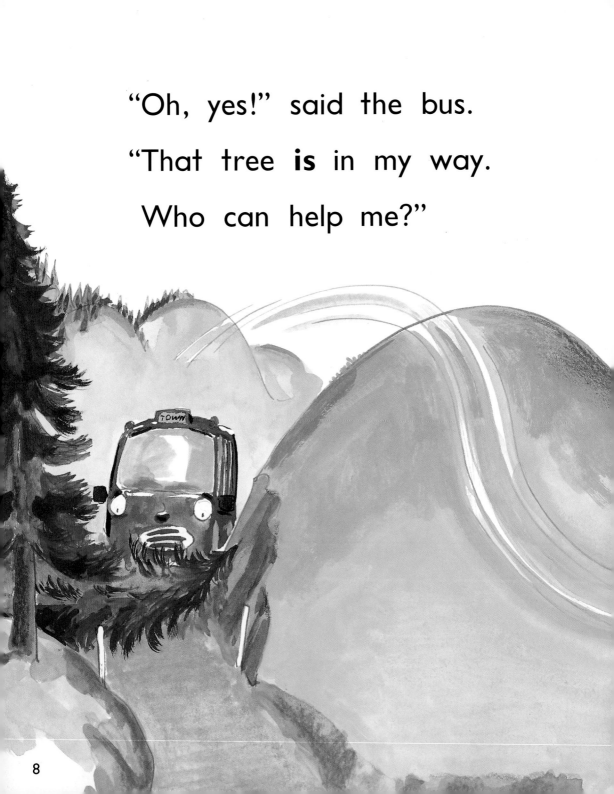

"I will go and get the bulldozer," said the helicopter.

"He is making a new road down by the river. He can help you."

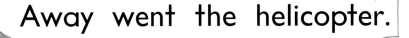

Away went the helicopter.

The helicopter came flying back to the bus.

"The bulldozer is coming now," he said.

"Oh, good!" said the bus.

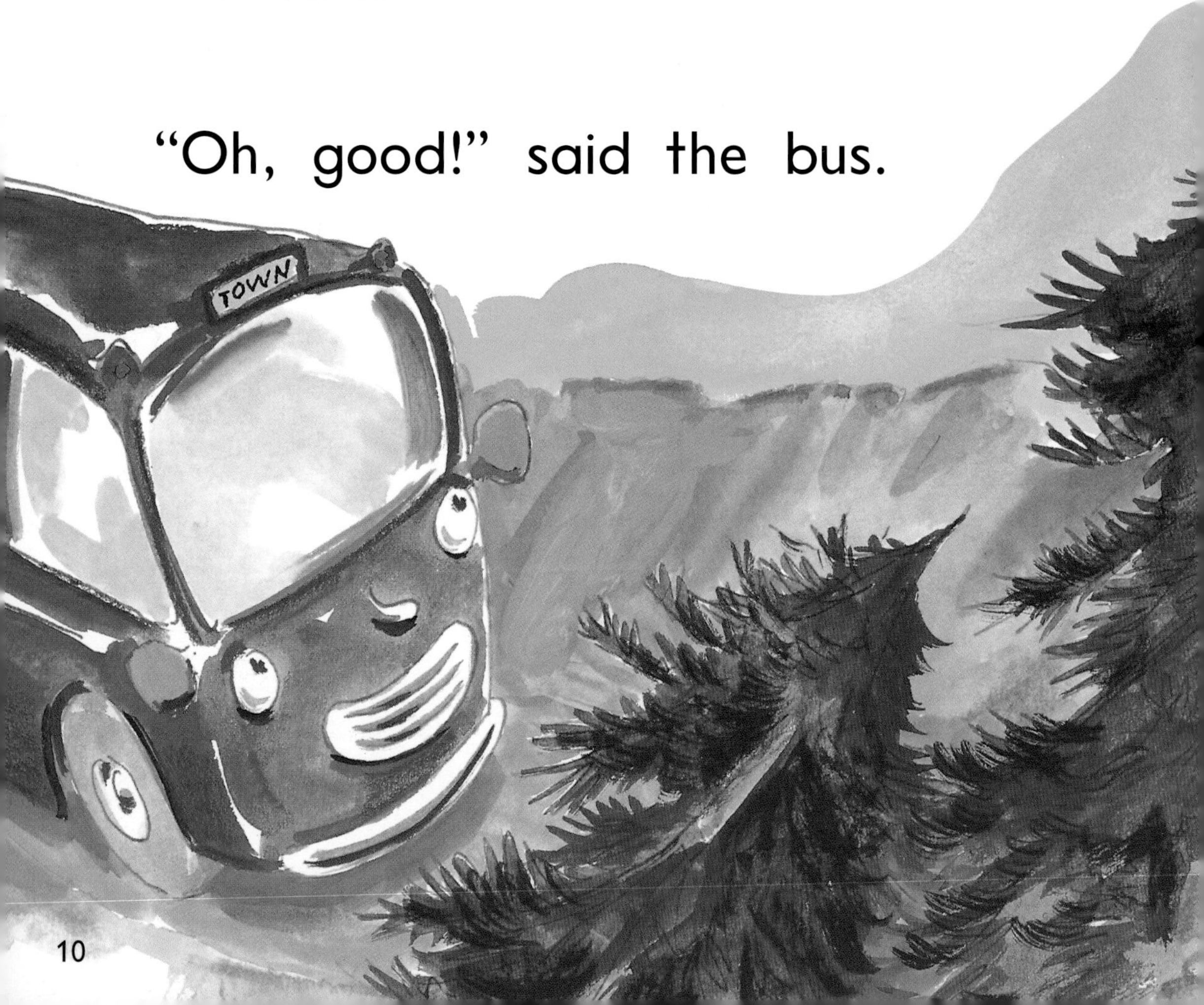
TOWN

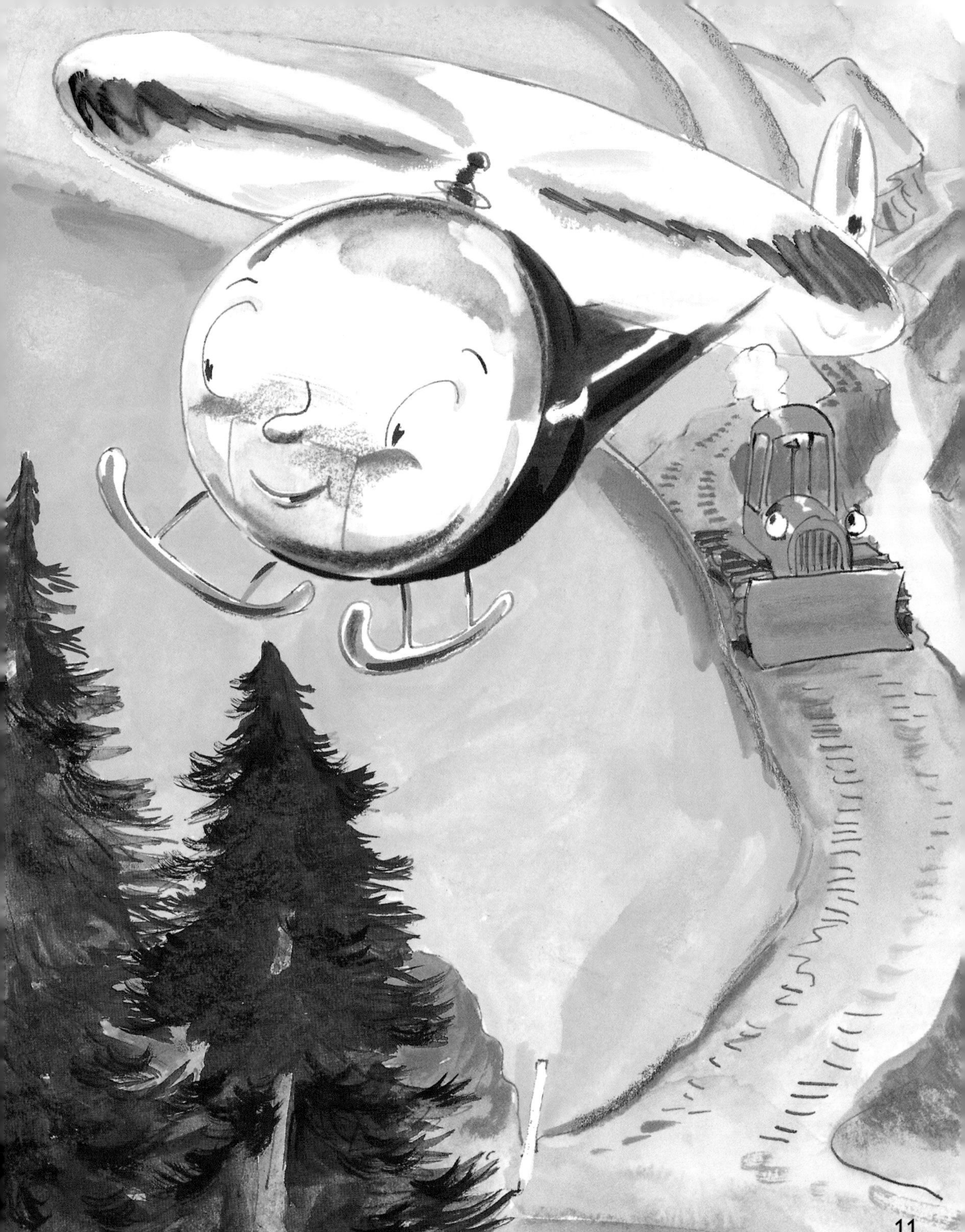

The bus said to the bulldozer,
"Look at that tree.
I can't get to town!"

"I can help you,"
said the bulldozer.

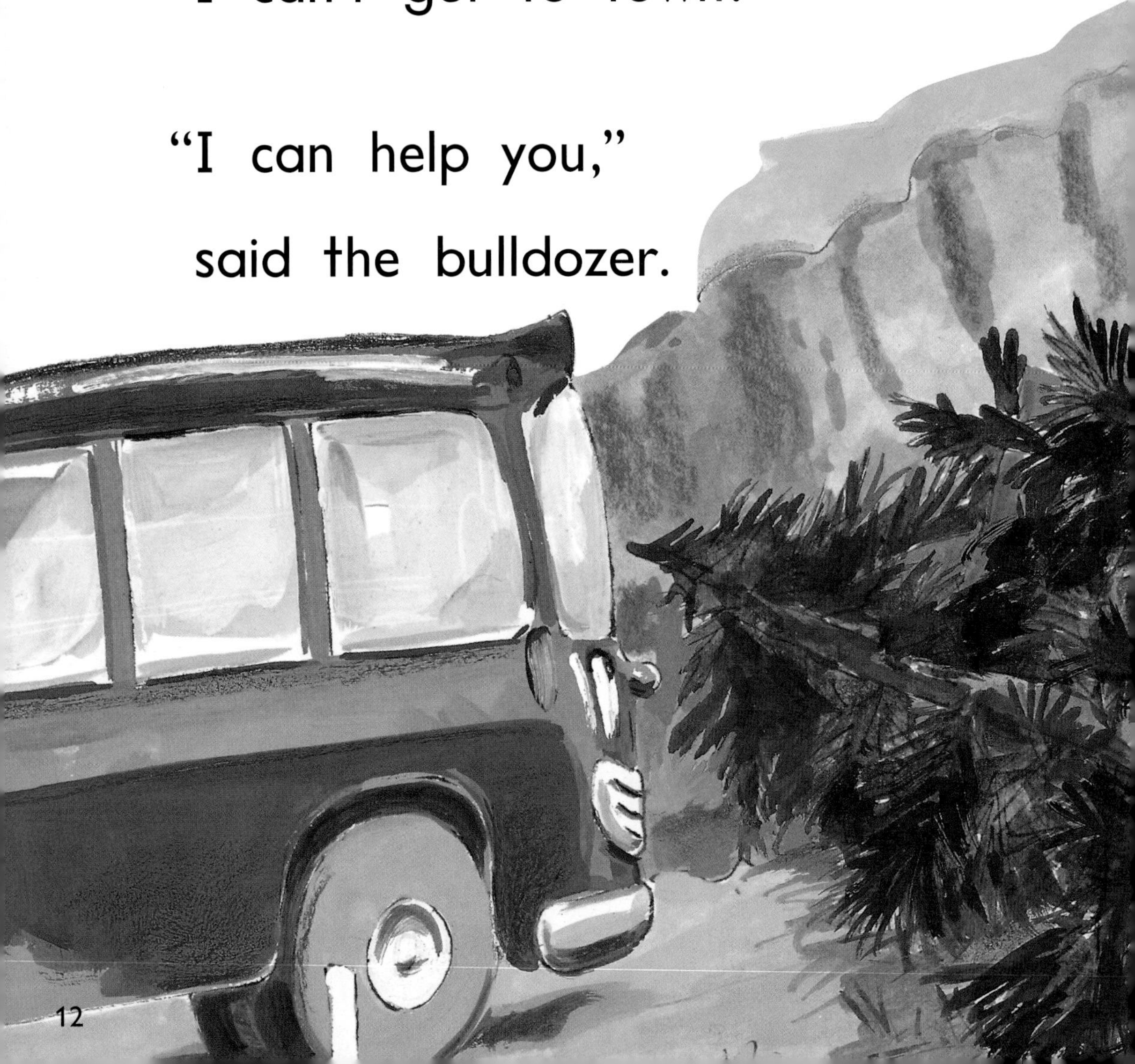

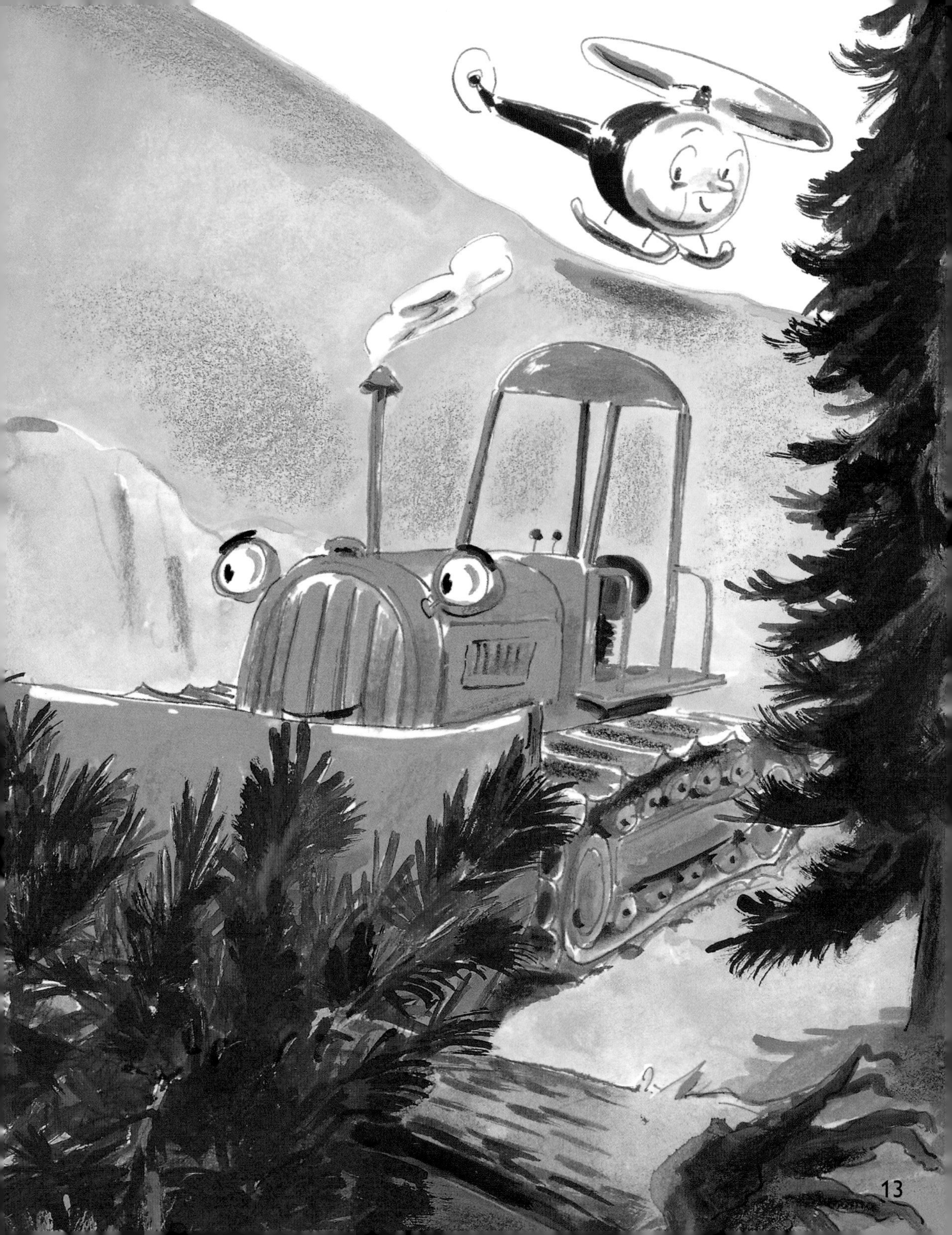

R-mmm! R-mmm!

went the bulldozer.

R-mmm! R-mmm!

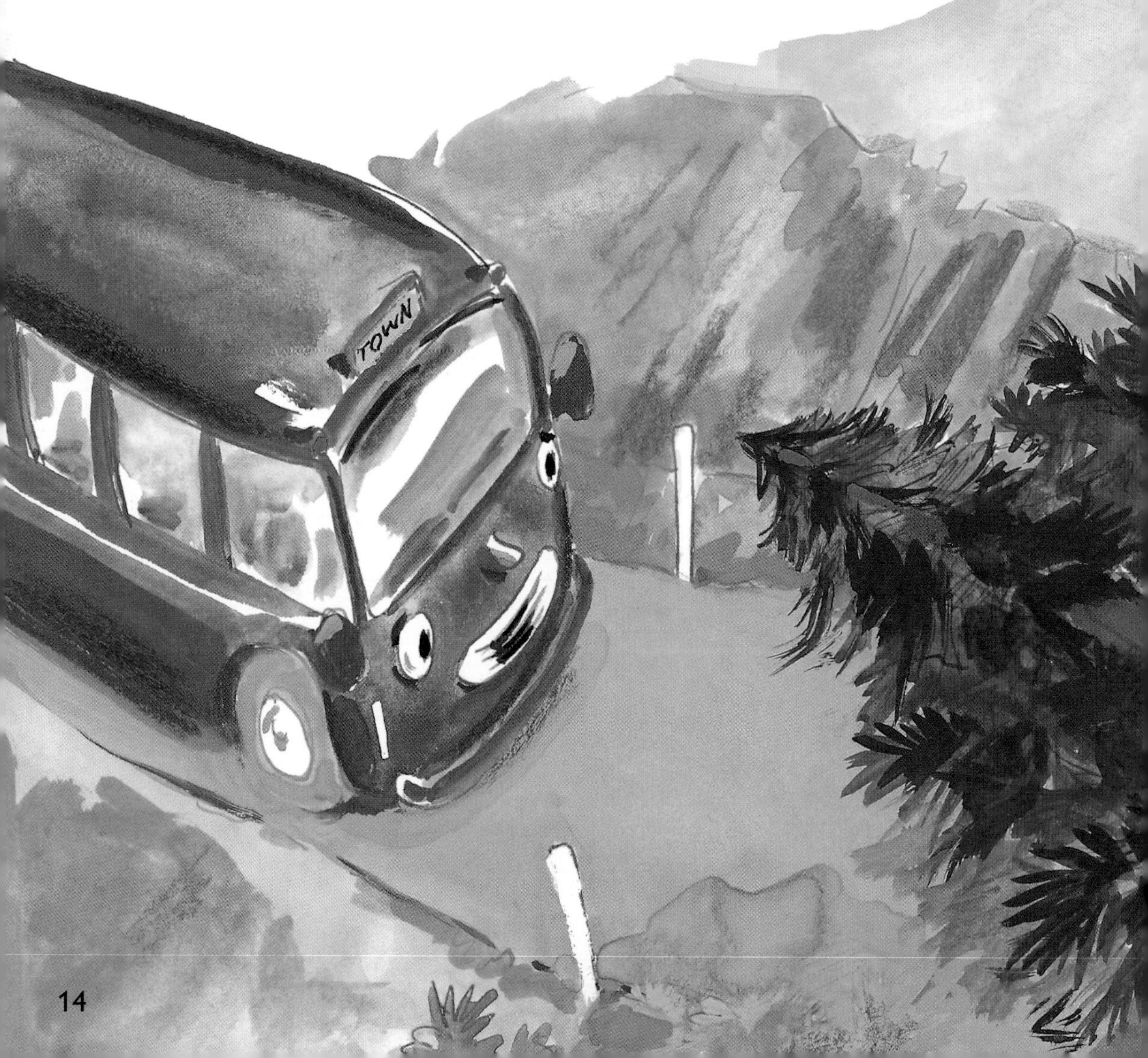
TOWN

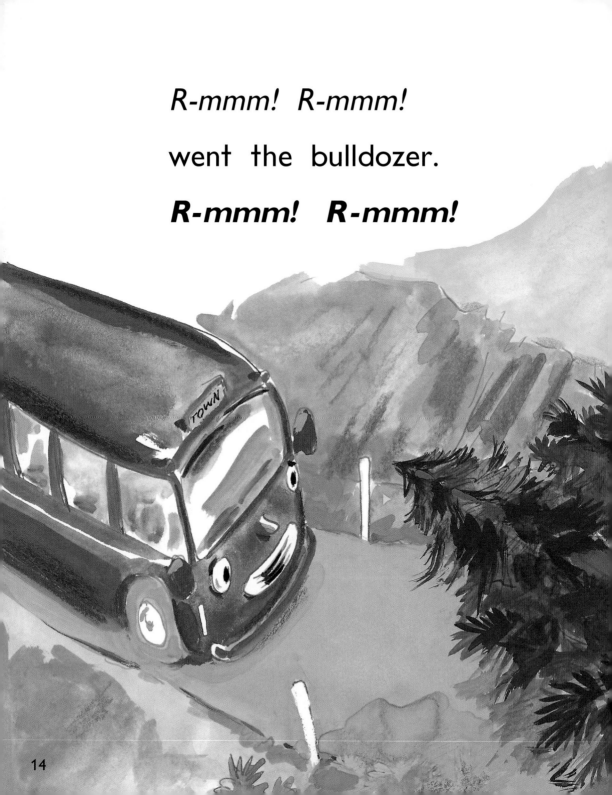

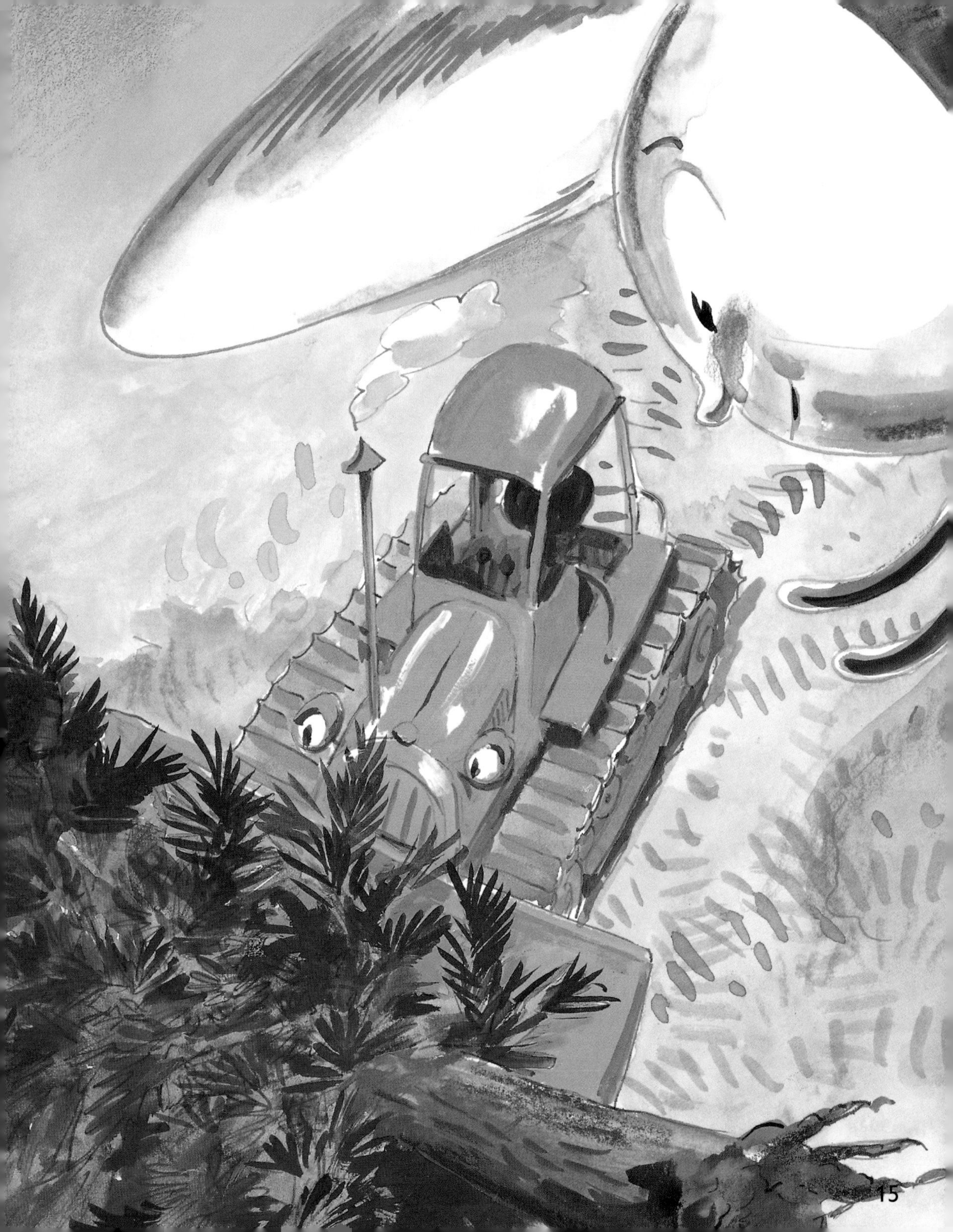

"The tree is out of the way,"
said the bulldozer,
"and now you can go to town."

"Oh, thank you!" said the bus.

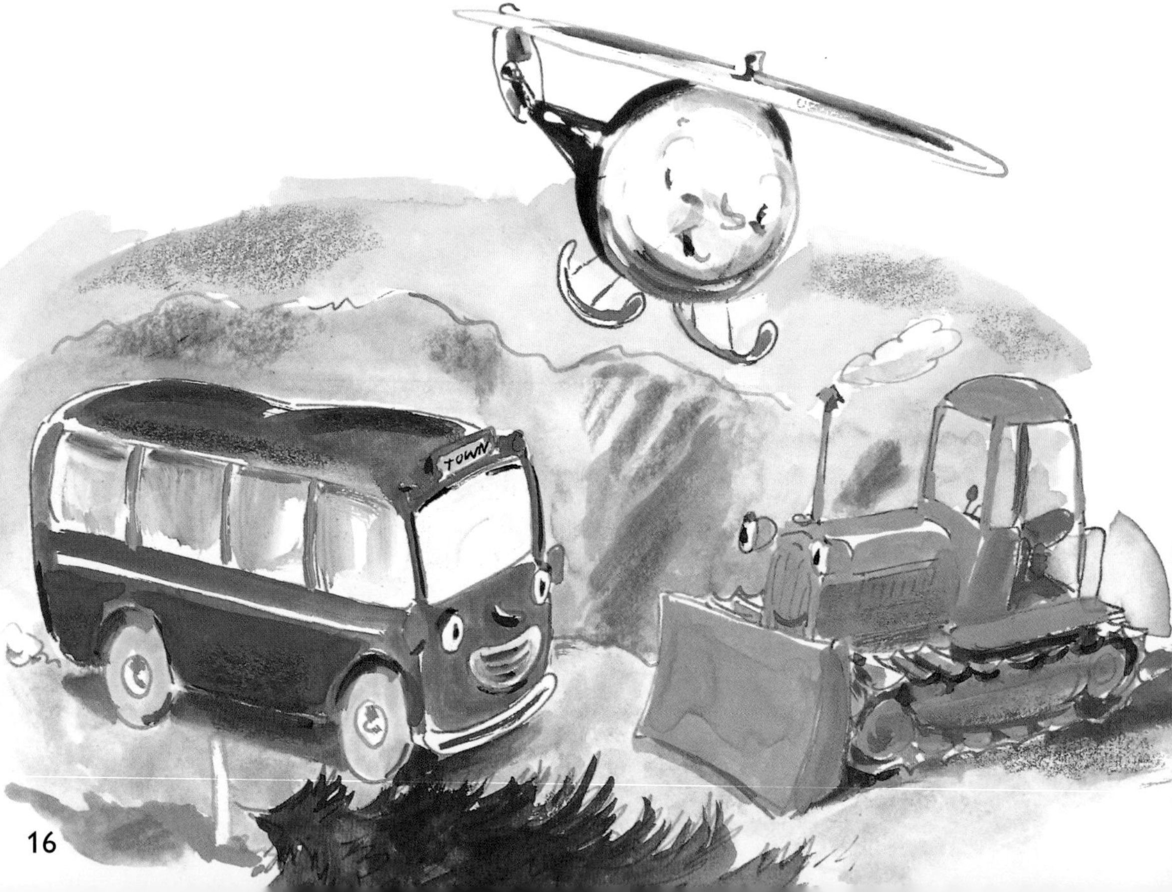
TOWN